T0115288

THE LITTLE BOOK OF
SELF-CARE
— FOR —
SCORPIO

*Simple Ways to Refresh
and Restore—According
to the Stars*

CONSTANCE STELLAS

ADAMS MEDIA

NEW YORK LONDON TORONTO SYDNEY NEW DELHI

Adams Media
An Imprint of Simon & Schuster, Inc.
100 Technology Center Drive
Stoughton, MA 02072

First Adams Media hardcover edition January 2019

ADAMS MEDIA and colophon are trademarks of Simon & Schuster.

For information about special discounts for bulk purchases, please contact Simon & Schuster Special Sales at 1-866-506-1949 or business@simonandschuster.com.

The Simon & Schuster Speakers Bureau can bring authors to your live event. For more information or to book an event contact the Simon & Schuster Speakers Bureau at 1-866-248-3049 or visit our website at www.simonspeakers.com.

Interior design by Colleen Cunningham
Interior images © Getty Images; Clipart.com

Manufactured in China

10 9 8

Library of Congress Cataloging-in-Publication Data has been applied for.

ISBN 978-1-5072-0978-3
ISBN 978-1-5072-0979-0 (ebook)

Dedication

To my fierce and transformative
Scorpio friends and clients, with respect.

CONTENTS

Acknowledgments

I would like to thank Karen Cooper and everyone at Adams Media who helped with this book. To Brendan O'Neill, Katie Corcoran Lytle, Sarah Doughty, Eileen Mullan, Casey Ebert, Sylvia Davis, and everyone else who worked on the manuscripts. To Frank Rivera, Colleen Cunningham, and Katrina Machado for their work on the book's cover and interior design. I appreciated your team spirit and eagerness to dive into the riches of astrology.

Introduction

It's time for you to have a little *"me" time*—powered by the zodiac. By tapping into your Sun sign's astrological and elemental energies, *The Little Book of Self-Care for Scorpio* brings star-powered strength and cosmic relief to your life with self-care guidance tailored specifically for you.

While you traditionally count on yourself for advice, Scorpio, this book gives you dozens of ideas to focus on your true self. This book provides information on how to incorporate self-care into your life while teaching you just how important astrology is to your overall self-care routine. You'll learn more about yourself as you learn about your sign and its governing element, water. Then you can relax, rejuvenate, and stay balanced with more than one hundred self-care ideas and activities perfect for your Scorpio personality.

From incorporating red ginseng into your daily routine to making patchouli your signature fragrance, you will find plenty of ways to heal your mind, body, and active spirit. Now, let the stars be your self-care guide!

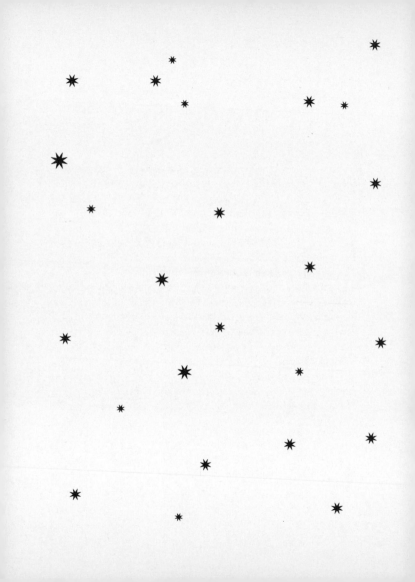

♏

PART 1

SIGNS, ELEMENTS, AND SELF-CARE

CHAPTER 1

WHAT IS SELF-CARE?

✳

Astrology gives insights into whom to love, when to charge forward into new beginnings, and how to succeed in whatever you put your mind to. When paired with self-care, astrology can also help you relax and reclaim that part of yourself that tends to get lost in the bustle of the day. In this chapter you'll learn what self-care is—for you. (No matter your sign, self-care is more than just lit candles and quiet reflection, though these activities may certainly help you find the renewal that you seek.) You'll also learn how making a priority of personalized self-care activities can benefit you in ways you may not even have thought of. Whether you're a Leo, a Pisces, or a Taurus, you deserve rejuvenation and renewal that's customized to your sign—this chapter reveals where to begin.

What Self-Care Is

Self-care is any activity that you do to take care of yourself. It rejuvenates your body, refreshes your mind, or realigns your spirit. It relaxes and refuels you. It gets you ready for a new day or a fresh start. It's the practices, rituals, and meaningful activities that you do, just for you, that help you feel safe, grounded, happy, and fulfilled.

The activities that qualify as self-care are amazingly unique and personalized to who you are, what you like, and, in large part, what your astrological sign is. If you're asking questions about what self-care practices are best for those ruled by water and born under the mysterious eye of Scorpio, you'll find answers—and restoration—in Part 2. But, no matter which of those self-care activities speak to you and your unique place in the universe on any given day, it will fall into one of the following self-care categories—each of which pertains to a different aspect of your life:

* Physical self-care
* Emotional self-care
* Social self-care
* Mental self-care
* Spiritual self-care
* Practical self-care

When you practice all of these unique types of self-care—and prioritize your practice to ensure you are choosing the best options for your unique sign and governing element—know that you are actively working to create the version of yourself that the universe intends you to be.

Physical Self-Care

When you practice physical self-care, you make the decision to look after and restore the one physical body that has been bestowed upon you. Care for it. Use it in the best way you can imagine, for that is what the universe wishes you to do. You can't light the world on fire or move mountains if you're not doing everything you can to take care of your physical health.

Emotional Self-Care

Emotional self-care is when you take the time to acknowledge and care for your inner self, your emotional well-being. Whether you're angry or frustrated, happy or joyful, or somewhere in between, emotional self-care happens when you choose to sit with your emotions: when you step away from the noise of daily life that often drowns out or tamps down your authentic self. Emotional self-care lets you see your inner you as the cosmos intend. Once you identify your true emotions, you can either accept them and continue to move forward on your journey or you can try to change any negative emotions for the better. The more you acknowledge your feelings and practice emotional self-care, the more you'll feel the positivity that the universe and your life holds for you.

Social Self-Care

You practice social self-care when you nurture your relationships with others, be they friends, coworkers, or family members. In today's hectic world it's easy to let relationships fall to the wayside, but it's so important to share your life with others—and let others share their lives with you. Social self-care is reciprocal and often karmic. The support and love that you put out into the universe through social self-care is given back to you by those you socialize with—often tenfold.

Mental Self-Care

Mental self-care is anything that keeps your mind working quickly and critically. It helps you cut through the fog of the day, week, or year and ensures that your quick wit and sharp mind are intact and working the way the cosmos intended. Making sure your mind is fit helps you problem-solve, decreases stress since you're not feeling overwhelmed, and keeps you feeling on top of your mental game—no matter your sign or your situation.

Spiritual Self-Care

Spiritual self-care is self-care that allows you to tap into your soul and the soul of the universe and uncover its secrets. Rather than focusing on a particular religion or set of religious beliefs, these types of self-care activities reconnect you with a higher power: the sense that something out there is bigger than you. When you meditate, you connect. When you pray, you connect. Whenever you do something that allows you to experience and marry yourself to the vastness that is the cosmos, you practice spiritual self-care.

Practical Self-Care

Self-care is what you do to take care of yourself, and practical self-care, while not as expansive as the other types, is made up of the seemingly small day-to-day tasks that bring you peace and accomplishment. These practical self-care rituals are important, but are often overlooked. Scheduling a doctor's appointment that you've been putting off is practical self-care. Getting your hair cut is practical self-care. Anything you can check off your list of things to be accomplished gives you a sacred space to breathe and allows the universe more room to bring a beautiful sense of cosmic fulfillment your way.

What Self-Care Isn't

Self-care is restorative. Self-care is clarifying. Self-care is whatever you need to do to make yourself feel secure in the universe.

Now that you know what self-care is, it's also important that you're able to see what self-care isn't. Self-care is not something that you force yourself to do because you think it will be good for you. Some signs are energy in motion and sitting still goes against their place in the universe. Those signs won't feel refreshed by lying in a hammock or sitting down to meditate. Other signs aren't able to ground themselves unless they've found a self-care practice that protects their cosmic need for peace and quiet. Those signs won't find parties, concerts, and loud venues soothing or satisfying. If a certain ritual doesn't bring you peace, clarity, or satisfaction, then it's not right for your sign and you should find something that speaks to you more clearly.

There's a difference though between not finding satisfaction in a ritual that you've tried and not wanting to try a self-care activity because you're tired or stuck in a comfort zone. Sometimes going to the gym or meeting up with friends is the self-care practice that you need to experience—whether engaging in it feels like a downer or not. So consider how you feel when you're actually doing the activity. If it feels invigorating to get on the treadmill or you feel delight when you actually catch up with your friend, the ritual is doing what it should be doing and clearing space for you—among other benefits...

The Benefits of Self-Care

The benefits of self-care are boundless and there's none that's superior to helping you put rituals in place to feel more at home in your body, in your spirit, and in your unique home in the cosmos. There are, however, other benefits to engaging in the practice of self-care that you should know.

Rejuvenates Your Immune System

No matter which rituals are designated for you by the stars, your sign, and its governing element, self-care helps both your body and mind rest, relax, and recuperate. The practice of self-care activates the parasympathetic nervous system (often called the rest and digest system), which slows your heart rate, calms the body, and overall helps your body relax and release tension. This act of decompression gives your body the space it needs to build up and strengthen your immune system, which protects you from illness.

Helps You Reconnect—with Yourself

When you practice the ritual of self-care—especially when you customize this practice based on your personal sign and governing element—you learn what you like to do and what you need to do to replenish yourself. Knowing yourself better, and allowing yourself the time and space that you need to focus on your personal needs and desires, gives you the gifts of self-confidence and self-knowledge. Setting time aside to focus on your needs also helps you put busy, must-do things aside, which gives you time to reconnect with yourself and who you are deep inside.

Increases Compassion

Perhaps one of the most important benefits of creating a self-care ritual is that, by focusing on yourself, you become more compassionate to others as well. When you truly take the time to care for yourself and make yourself and your importance in the universe a priority in your own life, you're then able to care for others and see their needs and desires in a new way. You can't pour from an empty dipper, and self-care allows you the space and clarity to do what you can to send compassion out into the world.

Starting a Self-Care Routine

Self-care should be treated as a ritual in your life, something you make the time to pause for, no matter what. You are important. You deserve rejuvenation and a sense of relaxation. You need to open your soul to the gifts that the universe is giving you, and self-care provides you with a way to ensure you're ready to receive those gifts. To begin a self-care routine, start by making yourself the priority. Do the customized rituals in Part 2 with intention, knowing the universe has already given them to you, by virtue of your sign and your governing element.

Now that you understand the role that self-care will hold in your life, let's take a closer look at the connection between self-care and astrology.

CHAPTER 2

SELF-CARE
AND ASTROLOGY

✳

Astrology is the study of the connection between the objects in the heavens (the planets, the stars) and what happens here on earth. Just as the movements of the planets and other heavenly bodies influence the ebb and flow of the tides, so do they influence you—your body, your mind, your spirit. This relationship is ever present and is never more important—or personal—than when viewed through the lens of self-care.

In this chapter you'll learn how the locations of these celestial bodies at the time of your birth affect you and define the self-care activities that will speak directly to you as a Leo, an Aries, a Capricorn, or any of the other zodiac signs. You'll see how the zodiac influences every part of your being and why ignoring its lessons can leave you feeling frustrated and unfulfilled. You'll also realize that, when you perform the rituals of self-care based on your sign, the wisdom of the cosmos will lead you down a path of fulfillment and restoration—to the return of who you really are, deep inside.

Zodiac Polarities

In astrology, all signs are mirrored by other signs that are on the opposite side of the zodiac. This polarity ensures that the zodiac is balanced and continues to flow with an unbreakable, even stream of energy. There are two different polarities in the zodiac and each is called by a number of different names:

* Yang/masculine/positive polarity
* Yin/feminine/negative polarity

Each polar opposite embodies a number of opposing traits, qualities, and attributes that will influence which self-care practices will work for or against your sign and your own personal sense of cosmic balance.

Yang

Whether male or female, those who fall under yang, or masculine, signs are extroverted and radiate their energy outward. They are spontaneous, active, bold, and fearless. They move forward in life with the desire to enjoy everything the world has to offer to them, and they work hard to transfer their inspiration and positivity to others so that those individuals may experience the same gifts that the universe offers them. All signs governed by the fire and air elements are yang and hold the potential for these dominant qualities. We will refer to them with masculine pronouns. These signs are:

* Aries
* Leo
* Sagittarius

* Gemini
* Libra
* Aquarius

There are people who hold yang energy who are introverted and retiring. However, by practicing self-care that is customized for your sign and understanding the potential ways to use your energy, you can find a way—perhaps one that's unique to you—to claim your native buoyancy and dominance and engage with the path that the universe opens for you.

Yin
Whether male or female, those who fall under yin, or feminine, signs are introverted and radiate inwardly. They draw people and experiences to them rather than seeking people and experiences in an extroverted way. They move forward in life with an energy that is reflective, receptive, and focused on communication and achieving shared goals. All signs governed by the earth and water elements are yin and hold the potential for these reflective qualities. We will refer to them with feminine pronouns. These signs are:

* Taurus
* Virgo
* Capricorn

* Cancer
* Scorpio
* Pisces

As there are people with yang energy who are introverted and retiring, there are also people with yin energy who are outgoing and extroverted. And by practicing self-care rituals that speak to your particular sign, energy, and governing body, you will reveal your true self and the balance of energy will be maintained.

Governing Elements

Each astrological sign has a governing element that defines their energy orientation and influences both the way the sign moves through the universe and relates to self-care. The elements are fire, earth, air, and water. All the signs in each element share certain characteristics, along with having their own sign-specific qualities:

* **Fire:** Fire signs are adventurous, bold, and energetic. They enjoy the heat and warm environments and look to the sun and fire as a means to recharge their depleted batteries. They're competitive, outgoing, and passionate. The fire signs are Aries, Leo, and Sagittarius.
* **Earth:** Earth signs all share a common love and tendency toward a practical, material, sensual, and economic orientation. The earth signs are Taurus, Virgo, and Capricorn.
* **Air:** Air is the most ephemeral element and those born under this element are thinkers, innovators, and communicators. The air signs are Gemini, Libra, and Aquarius.
* **Water:** Water signs are instinctual, compassionate, sensitive, and emotional. The water signs are Cancer, Scorpio, and Pisces.

Chapter 3 teaches you all about the ways your specific governing element influences and drives your connection to your cosmically harmonious self-care rituals, but it's important that you realize how important these elemental traits are to your self-care practice and to the activities that will help restore and reveal your true self.

Sign Qualities

Each of the astrological elements governs three signs. Each of these three signs is also given its own quality or mode, which corresponds to a different part of each season: the beginning, the middle, or the end.

* **Cardinal signs:** The cardinal signs initiate and lead in each season. Like something that is just starting out, they are actionable, enterprising, and assertive, and are born leaders. The cardinal signs are Aries, Cancer, Libra, and Capricorn.
* **Fixed signs:** The fixed signs come into play when the season is well established. They are definite, consistent, reliable, motivated by principles, and powerfully stubborn. The fixed signs are Taurus, Leo, Scorpio, and Aquarius.
* **Mutable signs:** The mutable signs come to the forefront when the seasons are changing. They are part of one season, but also part of the next. They are adaptable, versatile, and flexible. The mutable signs are Gemini, Virgo, Sagittarius, and Pisces.

Each of these qualities tells you a lot about yourself and who you are. They also give you invaluable information about the types of self-care rituals that your sign will find the most intuitive and helpful.

Ruling Planets

In addition to qualities and elements, each specific sign is ruled by a particular planet that lends its personality to those born under that sign. Again, these sign-specific traits give you valuable insight into the personality of the signs and the self-care rituals that may best rejuvenate them. The signs that correspond to each planet—and the ways that those planetary influences determine your self-care options—are as follows:

* **Aries:** Ruled by Mars, Aries is passionate, energetic, and determined.
* **Taurus:** Ruled by Venus, Taurus is sensual, romantic, and fertile.
* **Gemini:** Ruled by Mercury, Gemini is intellectual, changeable, and talkative.
* **Cancer:** Ruled by the Moon, Cancer is nostalgic, emotional, and home loving.
* **Leo:** Ruled by the Sun, Leo is fiery, dramatic, and confident.
* **Virgo:** Ruled by Mercury, Virgo is intellectual, analytical, and responsive.
* **Libra:** Ruled by Venus, Libra is beautiful, romantic, and graceful.
* **Scorpio:** Ruled by Mars and Pluto, Scorpio is intense, powerful, and magnetic.
* **Sagittarius:** Ruled by Jupiter, Sagittarius is optimistic, boundless, and larger than life.

* **Capricorn:** Ruled by Saturn, Capricorn is wise, patient, and disciplined.
* **Aquarius:** Ruled by Uranus, Aquarius is independent, unique, and eccentric.
* **Pisces:** Ruled by Neptune and Jupiter, Pisces is dreamy, sympathetic, and idealistic.

A Word on Sun Signs

When someone is a Leo, Aries, Sagittarius, or any of the other zodiac signs, it means that the sun was positioned in this constellation in the heavens when they were born. Your Sun sign is a dominant factor in defining your personality, your best self-care practices, and your soul nature. Every person also has the position of the Moon, Mercury, Venus, Mars, Jupiter, Saturn, Uranus, Neptune, and Pluto. These planets can be in any of the elements: fire signs, earth signs, air signs, or water signs. If you have your entire chart calculated by an astrologer or on an Internet site, you can see the whole picture and learn about all your elements. Someone born under Leo with many signs in another element will not be as concentrated in the fire element as someone with five or six planets in Leo. Someone born in Pisces with many signs in another element will not be as concentrated in the water element as someone with five or six planets in Pisces. And so on. Astrology is a complex system and has many shades of meaning. For our purposes looking at the self-care practices designated by your Sun sign, or what most people consider their sign, will give you the information you need to move forward and find fulfillment and restoration.

ESSENTIAL ELEMENTS: WATER

✳

Water is the fourth and final element of creation. It is essential for the planet and for our physical existence. It is amorphous, meaning it assumes the shape of its container or geographical location and solidifies only when frozen. Those who have water as their governing element—Cancer, Scorpio, and Pisces—all have a special energy signature and connection with water that guides all aspects of their lives. Water signs are intuitive and tend to live on waves of feeling. They are reflective, responsive, and fertile, and are often more sensitive than other signs. Their path in life is to quell their overwhelming emotions and use their instincts for love and compassion toward themselves and others.

Their approach to self-care must include these goals. Let's take a look at the mythological importance of water and its fluid counterparts, the basic characteristics of the three water signs, and what they all have in common when it comes to self-care.

The Mythology of Water

In Greek mythology water is linked to the god of the sea, Poseidon. Poseidon was brother to Zeus and Hades, and one of the six children conceived by Rhea and Cronos. His father, Cronos, ruled the universe, but was eventually overthrown by Zeus. After their father's collapse of power, Zeus, Hades, and Poseidon decided to divide the earth between the three of them. Poseidon became the lord of the sea, while Zeus became lord of Mount Olympus and sky, and Hades became the lord of the underworld.

The sea god was especially important in the ancient world as sea travel and navigation formed the principal trade and travel routes. Throughout mythology, going to sea was seen as a precarious adventure, and sailors often prayed to Poseidon for safe return and calm waters. Many myths feature Poseidon saving a ship at the last moment. In other myths he is not so merciful.

Like Poseidon, water signs make their decisions based off emotion. Their gut feelings guide them. This makes water signs highly compassionate and understanding, but it can also make them moody at times. Water signs may try to keep their emotions balanced in the hope of staying in control of their feelings, rather than allowing their feelings to control them. This desire drives their likes and dislikes, personality traits, and approaches to self-care.

The Element of Water

In terms of astrology, the water signs are called the feeling signs. They feel first, and think and speak later. They are very familiar with the emotional expression of tears, laughter, anger, joy, and grief. They often wear their heart on their sleeve and are extremely sentimental. Scorpio is somewhat of an exception to this characterization, but, nevertheless, she has a sensitive feeling mechanism. A water sign's energy moves inward, and they draw people and experiences to them rather than overtly seeking out people and experiences. For example, Scorpio's bravery means she is always open to new adventures. Cancer's loyalty encourages her to stick close to family and friends. And Pisces's creative intuition makes her a wonderful problem-solver when faced with a difficult conundrum.

Astrological Symbols

The astrological symbols (also called the zodiacal symbols) of the water signs also give you hints as to how the water signs move through the world. The symbols of all the water signs are creatures connected with the sea, the cradle of life:

* Scorpio is the Scorpion (and the Eagle and the Phoenix)
* Cancer is the Crab
* Pisces is the two Fish tied together

Scorpio has a complex set of symbols because there are varieties of scorpions, both in the sea and on land, but the sea is home to all these sensitive water signs. Scorpio uses her stinger to sting first rather than take the time to ask questions. Cancer the Crab holds on to her home tenaciously and never approaches anything directly. Instead, she moves from side to side to go forward in zigzag motions. And Pisces's two Fish tied together symbolize duality—one of the fish staying above the water, paying attention to the earth, and the other living in the sea, where dreams and the imagination rule.

Signs and Seasonal Modes

Each of the elements in astrology also has a sign that corresponds to a different part of each season.

* **Cardinal:** Cancer, as the first water sign, comes at the summer solstice, when summer begins. She is a cardinal sign and the leader of the water signs. She may lead indirectly, but has a powerful desire to be in control.
* **Fixed:** Scorpio, the next water sign, is a fixed water sign, and she rules when autumn is well established. The fixed signs are definite, motivated by principles, and powerfully stubborn.
* **Mutable:** And Pisces, the last water sign and the last sign of the zodiac, is a mutable sign. She moves us from winter to the spring equinox in Aries. The major characteristic of mutable, or changeable, signs is flexibility.

If you know your element and whether you are a cardinal, fixed, or mutable sign, you know a lot about yourself. This is invaluable for self-care and is reflected in the customized water sign self-care rituals found in Part 2.

Water Signs and Self-Care

Self-care comes naturally to water signs. Oftentimes, they find it is essential to take care of themselves because they feel acutely when something is askew inside them. They may complain bitterly about not feeling well, or about their sensitivities or the weather, but they generally know what to do to get back on course. Physical self-care is the hardest area for the water signs to master, because they do not like to do things unless they feel like doing them. Once they have a routine that has proven will make them feel better, they will stick to it, but before they adopt that routine, they are often hit-or-miss when it comes to diet, exercise, and medical checkups. Water signs are also very in tune with alternative cures and what their ancestors did for self-care.

Another essential factor in water sign self-care is the atmosphere of the gym or exercise location. Generally, water signs do not like crowds. If it is 5 p.m. and people are pounding out their aggressions from work on the treadmill, most water signs will choose to wait for the crowds to thin, or go earlier in the day. However, one of the great encouragements for water signs is the use of a shower or pool—a water source that they can include in their routine is a great enticement for water signs. Water signs may choose to attend classes at the gym, but most of the time they prefer to make sure that they are not overly influenced by other people's vibes.

Water signs are especially drawn to natural surroundings when it comes to self-care. Walking by a pond or lake is perhaps the best exercise for them, as it combines physical, mental, and spiritual practice. In a low-pressure environment, water signs feel that all their activities are worthwhile, both in terms of money and time. They are very aware of the money they spend and tend to be prudent and almost stingy with funds. And there is a direct relationship between their feeling of well-being and how much money they have in the bank.

Water signs are nurturers and make it a priority to take care of family and friends. It is always best for water signs to frame their self-care in terms of their familial feelings about something. For example, the statement "If you quit eating all this junk, you will help your family by setting a good example and you will feel better" is a winning one for water signs, marrying their love for their family with their own self-care. Once the water sign gets the feeling that they can extend the love and care of their family to themselves through self-care, they feel more comfortable designating attention to wellness practices.

In terms of emotional self-care, the most important factor for water signs is to avoid exaggerating their reactions to events or people. The more water signs can stay in the here and now, the less they will feel there are imaginary scenarios of people working against them. They are so sensitive that it is very easy for them to lapse into being self-conscious. A very good technique for water signs is to play a game asking themselves the question, "How would I feel if I were that person?" This thinking pattern encourages compassion rather than self-centeredness in water signs.

Water signs have a gift for feeling. In today's society we tend to diminish the importance of being emotional. Water signs may feel they have to do all the heavy lifting in the emotional department, which may make them feel lonely. Water signs are naturally empathetic, so the trick for them is to balance how they feel about other people and extend those good feelings to themselves. Feelings are different from intellectual, inspirational, and practical concerns. The water signs symbolize the potential of members of the human family to share their individual feelings.

So, now that you know what water signs need to practice self-care, let's look at each of the characteristics of Scorpio and how she can maintain her gifts.

CHAPTER 4

SELF-CARE FOR SCORPIO

*

Dates: October 23–November 21
Element: Water
Polarity: Yin
Quality: Fixed
Symbol: Scorpion, Eagle, Phoenix
Ruler: Mars, Pluto

Scorpio is the eighth sign of the zodiac and the third fixed sign of the zodiac. Like the other fixed signs that come in the middle of each season, she is strong, passionate, and stubborn. Scorpio is the strongest sign of the zodiac in terms of creative energy and her ability to transform herself, and she has a latent power that waits until it's needed to reveal itself. Scorpio meets the battle between the personality and the soul head-on throughout life.

Those born under this sign can experience the highest manifestations of this and the lowest: Scorpio is not a mild person; she is very magnetic and interested in the extremes of life.

Each astrological sign has a symbol. Scorpio has three: the Scorpion, the Eagle, and the Phoenix. The Scorpion represents the worst tendencies of this sign: an unevolved Scorpio who would rather sting herself to death than forego the pleasure of the sting. Here, we have a personality that can become locked into the "too much" syndrome: too much alcohol, sex, exercise, or dieting, too many drugs or too much discipline that cuts off the joy of life. Scorpio often passes through this phase and transforms her habits into helping others overcome addictions and find meaning in life. The second symbol is the Eagle: a bird representing spirit that can fly closer to the sun than any other and yet is also a fierce hunter. Here, Scorpio is moving from the low to the higher spiritual life. Scorpio's final symbol is the Phoenix: a mythical bird that rises from its ashes to create a new self. This quest of transformation is the one Scorpio aspires to, and self-care is a way that Scorpio can achieve this quest.

Scorpio has two planetary rulers: Mars and Pluto. Originally Scorpio was ruled by Mars, god of war, because of the fierce and strategic intensity astrologers observed with these personalities. Mars could be seen by the naked eye in ancient times and through observation was associated with Scorpio. In 1930, coincident with the development of atomic power, Pluto was discovered. Pluto is now considered the ruler of Scorpio because Pluto represents the transformation of the self at the deepest level. Pluto also represents riches including psychological, spiritual, and material which Scorpio craves.

In Roman mythology Pluto was the god of the underworld. He was a passionate god, and one deeply connected to the power, fecundity, and riches of the earth. *Pluto* in Latin means "the rich one," and, while the riches of Scorpio may not always be material, she is a very charismatic person who always has the wealth of her strength and focus to re-create herself. In Greek mythology Pluto was called Hades. One of Hades's powers was granting the use of a helmet that made the wearer invisible. Scorpio would love to have such an object. She loves being enigmatic and does not like to reveal herself to others.

Self-Care and Scorpio

Scorpio's focused energy must be expressed in creative activities, which are so important to this sign's self-care. Some unevolved Scorpios may linger on the darker side of life, but all are ultimately moving toward transformation. These descriptions may sound dramatic, but Scorpio isn't interested in living a superficial life. She wants to deal with the profound questions of life and death, head-on.

Scorpio does not reveal herself easily and is convinced that she is the best judge of what she needs, which makes it difficult for her to accept self-care advice from others. However, as a water sign, Scorpio is tuned into her body, mind, and spirit and can be a fount of knowledge about medicine, herbs, alternative cures, and a healthy lifestyle. She just needs to use this knowledge to prioritize herself and her needs.

Oftentimes, Scorpios are therapists, doctors, or counselors, and those born under this sign have a deep understanding of the world's ills. She is used to having others come to her and tell her all about their problems. Scorpio doesn't say anything, just listens, but after a short time, the other person might say, "Thanks, I feel a lot better." Scorpio has energetically helped them see something in a different way or transform their dark problems into the light. If Scorpio does this for herself, then there is no limit to the ingenious and successful ways she can pursue well-being and self-care.

One major area of self-care for most Scorpios is spending time engaging with pets. This very private sign has a wordless communication with animals that is healing and pleasurable. Scorpio also likes being a pet's master. Scorpio can be a very good animal trainer, or dog or horse whisperer. Pets offer uncomplicated love and Scorpio can return this.

Scorpio is usually able to easily incorporate sports into her self-care programs. She recognizes the need to move her energy around and keep it moving. Water sports (for this water sign) and martial arts are good choices. Taking a POUND class or moving to a drumbeat speaks to the primitive part of Scorpio. The social aspect of sports has limited appeal for Scorpio. Scorpio is sometimes solitary and may enjoy long-distance or endurance sports.

Psychological health is entirely up to Scorpio. Unless she decides to seek help or sees the need, she sees no point to counseling. And a therapist must be as complex and strong as the Scorpio client for any therapy to work. The most important part of a therapeutic relationship is that it allows spiritual, even religious, growth. Scorpio isn't fooling around this lifetime. She wants to purify her soul and will work with anyone who can offer that kind of growth.

Scorpio Rules the Reproductive System and Organs of Elimination

Scorpio rules the reproductive organs as well as the organs of elimination, basically everything from the navel to the tops of the thighs. This is the powerhouse of the body, the root and sacral chakras in yoga. Problems with the reproductive organs can sometimes mean that there is an energy block in the body. In addition to seeking medical advice, Scorpio might consider yoga exercises to keep this area of the body relaxed and unblocked. However, Scorpio must beware of satisfying her desires without thinking about the consequences. Even for the sign ruled by the reproductive organs, there is a difference between healthy sex and wanton sex for power.

The elimination organs are not as much fun to consider but essential for the body's health. Keeping the colon and urinary tract healthy ensures that impurities can be eliminated from the body. Those born under this sign might ask her doctor about taking probiotics, which keep the balance of flora constant in the body. A Scorpio woman might consider asking her doctor about taking a daily dose of cranberry juice, which may help ensure that the urinary tract remains healthy.

Scorpio and Self-Care Success

One major pitfall for Scorpio's self-care program is that Scorpio sometimes confuses care with pleasure. Everything that feels good isn't necessarily self-care, which can be difficult for this water sign to accept. If Scorpio spirals into a cycle of self-destructive activity, it will take some time for her to recoup and find herself on the side of light. But that is the power of this sign; more than any other sign she can pull herself from the depths and make a truly remarkable transformation.

Another pitfall for Scorpio's self-care program is the very opposite of the first. Scorpio can become so rigid and obsessive about self-care that there is no flow to life or spontaneity.

Too much discipline is too much control, and eventually there is a rebellion. When Scorpio follows her instincts and moderates her extremes, she is able to practice self-care to her best ability.

The most successful aspect of self-care for Scorpio is her desire to engage in these types of rituals. Once she decides on a program, a routine, or practice, she will continue it until it no longer serves her. Her motivation is simple: "I create a healthier me." This is why Scorpio will not benefit from a quick fix. She wants to understand the root of the problem, be it physical, mental, or spiritual. Meditation, spiritual practices, dance, and exercise are all ways she can move her considerable energy into balance so she heals herself and provides self-care.

Humor is a big factor in Scorpio's outlook on life. She has a biting wit and is often sarcastic, but wildly funny. Laughing at the world—and at herself—is a good self-care practice and a way of sharing with other people. Scorpio can be a loner and sharing a joke is a way to keep connected.

Whether she's laughing, engaging in physical activity, or looking for a creative space, Scorpio, like all water signs, is intuitive. And she uses this trait when deciding which self-care rituals are right for her, which is why it is imperative for her to make her self-care choices based on her astrological sign. So let's take a look at some self-care activities that are tailored specifically for you, Scorpio.

♏

PART 2

SELF-CARE
RITUALS
— FOR —
SCORPIO

Treat Yourself to
Tiger's Eye Jewelry

Scorpio is fiercely loyal and very brave, but she also has a tendency to be intense. Keep grounded in tumultuous situations by wearing tiger's eye jewelry. Due to her passionate nature, Scorpio must always focus on staying centered. While it can be difficult to do so at times, carrying or wearing tiger's eye is an easy way to keep emotions in check.

It represents a wise, all-knowing eye and brings clarity to an individual's vision—essential when trying to keep a level head during emotional times.

Get Motivated

If you find that you are feeling unmotivated to work out, start by listening to your favorite music to get amped up. Sometimes just feeling the beat can jump-start your energy level and get your blood flowing. If you are working out at home, you may even want to try dancing around as your entire workout. Dancing for 30 minutes is great cardio. Just blast your favorite tunes and let your body move naturally. Mix up the playlist tempo to keep things interesting. No slow songs allowed!

Stay Healthy with Red Ginseng

I mmunity is important for all of us, but is particularly essential for Scorpio for a couple of reasons. First, Scorpio rules over the elimination organs. Keeping the colon and urinary tract healthy ensures that impurities can be eliminated from the body. Second, Scorpio sometimes has a hard time expressing emotions. During times when she feels sad or angry, she can turn inward, and her emotional unrest can affect her physical well-being.

Boost your immune system by taking red ginseng. Not only does it have anti-inflammatory and anti-oxidant effects, but it is claimed it also strengthens the immune system and can help fight fatigue. Ask your doctor (who is familiar with your health and medications) about making red ginseng a part of your self-care routine on a short-term basis either by enjoying a cup of tea or taking a supplement. It's an easy way for Scorpio to keep wellness at the top of her mind.

Collect Glass Figurines

Scorpio is the ruler of transformation, a characteristic that makes her appreciate transformation in other beings and objects.

If you'd like to bring a talisman of transformation into your home, consider collecting clear glass figurines or abstract shapes and placing them by a source of natural light. As you enjoy the rainbow that the sun makes when shining on the figures, note the transformation that is happening right before your eyes. When the light hits the glass and causes it to bend, the light is transformed into a rainbow. Pause and take a moment to appreciate the transformative beauty and power.

Get Away from It All...

In the swamps! While it may not sound like your typical vacation, consider visiting a swamp. A water sign, Scorpio rules all swamplands, so in a way you'd be visiting your own kingdom.

The next time you'd like to take some time away, consider a high-speed fan boat adventure in New Orleans. Or head down under and take a floatplane to Australia's remote Finniss River floodplains. Or, off the coast of the Bulgarian Black Sea, discover Alepu, a swamp and nature reserve home to a large variety of rare waterbirds.

Exploring these swamplands will satisfy your adventurous side, and you may find you'll feel at home at these mysteriously beautiful and watery places.

Choose Flowing Exercises

As a water sign, you are drawn to fluid movements. When it comes to exercise, look for things that give your body freedom to move in the way it wants to. The last thing you want is to be restrained. Try tai chi or an aerobic dance class. Even Pilates can be soothing for water signs, as it helps build muscle and keeps you moving in a natural way.

Stick to a Routine

——————

Routine can be boring for a water sign, but it is key to a solid self-care regimen. It may take discipline to stick to a routine, but without a well-constructed plan, apathy will take over and you'll find yourself doing nothing to improve your overall wellness. Make sure you vary your activities to keep things fresh and new. It may help to buy a large desk calendar and mark off when you are doing what activity. This will help keep you on track and will take any indecisiveness off the table.

Carry Tourmaline

S corpio is the eighth sign of the zodiac and the third fixed sign of the zodiac. The fixed signs come in the middle of each season; they are strong, passionate, and stubborn. All the fixed signs partake of serpent or kundalini power. In Scorpio this power waits within until needed. If you ever need a reminder of how powerful you are, consider carrying a tourmaline crystal.

A tourmaline crystal in your left pocket promotes a sense of power and self-confidence. It can empower you during challenging times, when you may most need a reminder of your innate power. It is also an excellent crystal for meditation, and for promoting healing.

Keep one close at hand to help ensure you are capitalizing on your power as a Scorpio.

Make Water a Part of Your Life

You may think that all water signs are naturally drawn to water in every capacity, but this isn't necessarily true. Every water sign is different and has different preferences. While most water signs take comfort in water-based activities, such as swimming, diving, and water aerobics, others prefer to simply be near water, but not in it. Wherever you fall on this spectrum, water is an important grounding mechanism for you. It calms you, makes you feel safe, and helps orient you when you are feeling lost. Make water a part of your life in whatever way you feel most comfortable.

Stretch

―――――――――

The type of exercise you do as a water sign is very important. Many water signs have smooth muscles that do not usually bulk up, so doing exercises that are designed to add heft to your muscle won't be particularly beneficial. Instead, you should look for exercises that stretch your muscles, such as yoga. You don't even have to go to a yoga class to try it out. There are plenty of online videos for beginner yogis to try—just stick to the basics.

If yoga isn't your favorite, you can still make stretching an essential part of your wellness routine by stretching before and after every workout. It may even help to do some gentle stretches before bed to keep your muscles limber and flexible.

Watch Your Salt (and Water)

———————

You've probably heard that our bodies are made up of more than 50 percent water. Water signs tend to hold on to water more than other signs do, which means they often have a softness to their faces and bodies. It may seem counterproductive, but drinking the right amount of water daily may, in certain circumstances, help reduce water retention, as well as flush toxins. Sometimes our bodies retain water in response to dehydration. Try to meet the recommended guidelines for how much water you should drink every day (depending on sex, lifestyle, climate, and health).

You can also watch how much salt you consume. Too much sodium (either in table salt or processed foods and soft drinks) increases your risk of water retention. If you do experience water retention symptoms, visit your doctor for advice.

Gain Clarity with Malachite

Scorpio is strong and passionate. But with these strengths sometimes comes stubbornness. Keep your head cool and clear by keeping malachite close at hand.

While toxic in its unfinished state, when polished and finished, it is commonly used in the creation of figurines or jewelry. Additionally, it is very good for Scorpio clarity, transforming animal nature into productivity and creativity. During times of frustration, when you may veer toward stubbornness, wear your malachite jewelry, or focus on a malachite figure or talisman. It will help you to clear your head so you can proceed without your judgment clouded.

Respect Snakes

Do you cringe when you see a picture of a snake? Consider changing your opinion of your serpent sister.

Ruled by Scorpio, snakes symbolize the transformative life force that Scorpio has. Just as a snake can shed her skin, so too can Scorpio transform her being. Rather than fearing these slithery creatures, reflect on how alike you are. Scorpio desires growth, rebirth, and metamorphosis. Scorpio is not afraid of reaching deep within herself to summon change and encourage soul transformation. Even though you may not want to have a pet as a snake, next time you think of your spiritual sister, respect your commonalities.

Beautify Your Kitchen with Apothecary Jars

Scorpio rules all pharmacists and medical equipment. Honor your spirit and give a nod to this alignment by keep grains and spices in apothecary jars.

Scorpio makes a wonderful pharmacist or physician, since these careers combine passions, essential medical knowledge, and personal interactions aimed to benefit others. While it might not be the perfect job for you personally, you can give a nod to this part of your Scorpio nature by decorating your home with apothecary décor. The kitchen is the easiest space to accomplish this in, though you can also find appropriate furniture for your bedroom or living room—interesting bureaus and shelves that hearken back to a time before modern pharmacy practice. Whenever you beautify your space, you are performing an act of self-care, and also setting the stage for those times in the future when you can relax and enjoy your space.

Turn to Nature

Stress happens to everyone; it's how you handle it that makes a difference. For water signs the best way to beat stress is to retreat to a safe space: nature. If you have the opportunity to spend time by a body of water, like a creek, river, or, ideally, the beach, do so as often as possible. Just listen to the sound the water makes as it moves, lapping against rocks or sand, and let the stress melt away from your muscles. If you don't have easy access to a body of water, download and listen to some water sounds outside. It's not quite the same, but it will mimic the calming experience of being by the water.

Laugh As Much As Possible

L aughter can soothe the soul, especially the soul of a weary water sign. You tend to feel deeply, and need a healthy release to let go of those heavy emotions. Laughter can be that release. If you don't laugh, you may start to get bogged down with too many negative feelings. The only way to survive in life is to see the comedy in things. Water signs are especially good at this, but, sometimes, they need a little push. When you are feeling down, go to a funny movie or seek out a stand-up comedian putting on a show.

Avoid Crowds

—————————

You are a sensitive soul, water sign, one who tends to absorb the vibrations and energy coming from other people. Because of this, it's best for you to avoid large crowds, especially if you are feeling vulnerable or sad. Being in a large group of strangers will just exacerbate those negative feelings you are struggling with, and may even make you feel more alone than you already do. Instead, stay home and allow yourself some quality relaxation time. Give yourself permission to lounge around and be lazy. Enjoy your own company!

Visit a Labyrinth

_____

Scorpio always rises to a challenge, and enjoys the complex and mysterious. Why not add a little fun to your self-care and visit a maze?

Simultaneously fun and exhilarating, mazes are a great way to add mystery to your day, without any drama. Get a group of friends together and make it a competition—who can escape first? Or go on your own for a personal challenge. Either way, you will leave feeling accomplished and inspired.

Wash It Off

As a water sign, you are used to being affected by other people's energy and the energy of the atmosphere around you. It is essential for your emotional health that you wash away any feelings you may have absorbed from others throughout the day. Make a point to take a shower or bath every night to cleanse your emotional aura. You may even find dry brushing before you bathe to be beneficial. Not only does dry brushing help loosen and remove dead skin from your body, it can be a wonderfully cathartic experience for water signs, especially if you envision the ritual as also sloughing away any emotional burdens you have picked up over the past few hours.

Adopt a Ferret

_____

Scorpio is typically very private, and has a wordless communication with animals. Their relationship not only is enjoyable, but can also be healing. Pets offer uncomplicated love and Scorpio can return this.

If you're considering adopting a pet, why not try a ferret? A ferret may be an unusual pet, but their cuteness and strangeness are perfect for Scorpio. A less common choice than a cat or dog, this very active animal can be a wonderful companion for you. Additionally, they love to play, which can add a spirited and fun element to your daily care. Just make sure to get expert advice on adopting (and properly caring for) your ferret from a local animal shelter before you commit.

Keep It Simple

_____

When it comes to fashion, water signs like to keep things simple and classic. Their favorite colors for clothing are muted tones, like navy blue, black, gray, and white, along with pops of color, like turquoise. Once a water sign finds a style that they are comfortable with, they'll stick to it. Changing their style requires a lot of energy, so it's easier for them to stay with what works.

Don't be surprised if it takes you a little while to get acclimated to a new fashion accessory or style of dressing. If you get the urge, though, do try out something new. You can always go back to your favorite staple items if you are uncomfortable.

Set Good Bathroom Vibes

M ake your bathroom into the oasis you deserve! Having the perfect vessel to indulge your watery tendencies is essential for a water sign's self-care. Invest in a deep tub for your bathroom that you can soak in when you are feeling stressed—the deeper and roomier the better. Buy luxurious bubble baths and bath bombs to use when you draw a bath. Additionally, make sure that you have good water pressure for your shower. Lastly, choose bathroom tile that reflects water themes and colors, such as light blue, white, and green.

Enjoy Flamenco Music

———————

If you haven't tried listening to flamenco music before, you may be missing out. The rhythmic qualities of this Spanish-based music speak to Scorpio's passionate soul.

Flamenco music can be part of your self-care routine in a myriad of ways. You can use it to unwind at the end of a stressful day, or make it part of your physical fitness regimen and use it as the soundtrack of your dance-based workout. If you're feeling daring, why not try flamenco dancing on a date? The sensual music can be both soothing and seductive.

Do Nighttime Activities

Some water signs are morning people, but most thrive in the nighttime hours. That's because the night calls to water signs. It is dark and peaceful, and they often feel that they are protected when the sun is down. If you are feeling vulnerable, plan a nighttime activity, such as stargazing, watching fireworks, or going for a simple drive or walk around your neighborhood with a friend. The key is to take some time to appreciate the quiet and calm that come with the evening hours, allowing the shift from chaotic day to tranquil night to ease your mind.

Sail Off to Sleep

Fortunately, water signs tend to fall asleep relatively easily, but they can sometimes become distracted if their environment isn't conducive to sleep. At night it's beneficial to use room-darkening curtains to keep any light from creeping in. Water signs like to sleep in complete darkness, and may even find it difficult to sleep if their room isn't pitch black. Using blackout shades and dark heavy curtains will help make your bedroom cozy and dark, just the way water signs like it. Alternatively, you may consider using a sleeping mask to prevent any light from bothering you while you sleep.

Add Alexandrite to
Your Jewelry Collection

One of Scorpio's ruling planets is Mars: the red planet. Due to its red color, a beautiful stone for Scorpio is alexandrite.

Compared to many gemstones, alexandrite's discovery was relatively recent as it was found only in the last 200 years. Despite this, it has already gained a reputation as having mystical properties. One possible reason for this is that the miners who originally discovered the stone reported that it changed color from green to red, depending on the light. Its red shade is often described as fiery, and can be a beautiful addition to Scorpio's wardrobe.

Visit a Native American Reservation

S corpio is naturally curious and has a deep respect for history. Capitalize on this by visiting a Native American reservation.

Across the United States, you will find reservations you can visit to learn about the Native American experience. Scorpio will find she has an affinity for the indigenous people, and these reservations are the ideal settings for learning and appreciating their history.

While there, take full advantage of your natural talent as a good listener, and open your eyes and ears to Native American people who would like to share their stories with you.

Get Cozy

There's nothing quite like taking a long bath or shower and then snuggling up in a thick bath towel. For water signs self-care means pampering yourself with luxury whenever you can. A simple way to do this is to invest in high-quality towels or a robe that you can wear after you've washed away any negative emotions from the day. The soft, fluffy material will help you feel safe and protected. If you have the opportunity, consider buying a towel warmer as well.

Go It Alone

———————

When it comes to sports and leisure, water signs tend to do best with activities that take place outside and don't involve a lot of people. This means that team sports aren't always the best option for you. Water signs should avoid recreational leagues that attract a lot of people. Instead, they do better with low-pressure activities that focus on nature, such as walking, hiking, and climbing. You may find that you, as a water sign, don't really like competition, and there's absolutely nothing wrong with that.

Find an activity out in nature that suits you best. If you feel like you want some company, invite a few trusted friends along to join you.

Listen to the Music of Your
Scorpio Brothers and Sisters

A s a water sign, Scorpio is naturally creative, and it comes as no surprise that many musical artists were born under the Scorpio sign.

Expand your playlist and take a listen to the many songs of Scorpios who create music in all genres, from rock to rap to country to folk to pop, including:

* Drake (born October 24)
* Katy Perry (born October 25)
* Keith Urban (born October 26)
* Brad Paisley (born October 28)
* Frank Ocean (born October 28)
* Red Hot Chili Peppers (front man Anthony Kiedis was born November 1)
* Joni Mitchell (born November 7)
* Diplo (born November 10)
* Jeff Buckley (born November 17)
* Björk (born November 21)

Treat Yourself to Sexy Nightwear

Every astrological sign rules a certain area of the body. For Scorpio, this includes the genitals. Naturally passionate and intense, Scorpio enjoys spicing things up in the bedroom. Why not set the stage for an exciting and romantic evening with your partner by showing up in sexy lingerie or nightwear?

Experiment with bold colors such as black or red, and alluring, silky fabrics. Make your bedroom an ideal setting for romance by dimming the lights and dressing your bed in lush fabrics. Enjoy your partner, and your time together. Self-care can be mutually enjoyable.

Get Cooking

Cooking and baking are wonderful outlets for water signs, though when given the choice, they tend to stick to the basics they've already mastered rather than experiment with new recipes. After all, if you have a handful of staple dishes that you know you can create easily and well, why would you want to try something new and risk it tasting terrible? Comfort food in particular appeals to a hungry water sign. Everything from macaroni and cheese to mashed potatoes and pancakes are usually big hits. So, why not keep your experimentation to your preferences, and buy a comfort food cookbook that can help expand your repertoire of recipes?

Take a Beach Vacation

Indulge the innate connection you have to water by taking a vacation to an island or near a beach. Being by the water will help recharge your batteries when you are feeling depleted. The warm weather in most tropical locations is perfect for a water sign who is hoping to lounge by the beach or pool and let their worries fade away.

Look for vacation destinations that also include water activities, such as lessons in paddle boarding or snorkeling, to help you connect with your element. If you can swing an all-inclusive resort, you'll get even more bang for your buck, with food, lodging, entertainment, and drinks included.

Find Some Privacy

Y ou may have noticed that, as a water sign, you
need quiet and privacy to get your work done.
When it comes to your job, you will be more productive
working in a cubicle or by yourself than in an open-plan
office or large group. You tend to get overwhelmed
when you have too many people around you, so when
you really need to concentrate, try retreating to your
own secluded space. This will help keep you away from
all the hustle and bustle, and limit your distractions.

When you feel the need to talk to others, a
communal kitchen or break room is your ideal space.
This is where you can comfortably mingle with
coworkers before going back to your cubbyhole to
get some work done. If you have a job where a group
environment is highly valued, try speaking to your
supervisor and letting them know how you work best.
You might be surprised by how understanding they
will be!

Immerse Yourself in the Works of Scorpio Artists

An afternoon in the museum can be a simultaneously relaxing and inspiring act of self-care. Next time you have the opportunity to spend some time admiring great works of art, pay particular attention to artists born under the Scorpio sign. A few notables include:

* Pablo Picasso (born October 25)
* Roy Lichtenstein (born October 27)
* Claude Monet (born November 14)
* Georgia O'Keeffe (born November 15)

If you're unable to visit a museum, check out their works online. If you're particularly drawn to one artist, consider decorating your home with prints of their work—a tribute to a fellow Scorpio.

Surround Yourself in the Scent of Myrrh

S corpio likes to have a mysterious scent in the atmosphere. While you may have a particular incense or candle that you love, consider trying myrrh.

Myrrh has an earth scent. Some people say it resembles black licorice. It also has spiritual significance, often being used in prayer or meditation.

Consider burning some during quiet, meditative moments, perhaps prior to retiring to bed or when you need to focus and recharge. Creating an atmosphere of calm and staying in touch with your thoughts and emotions is an important aspect of self-care.

Seek Out a Sauna
or Steam Room

The benefits of a sauna or steam room go far beyond simple stress relief. Sitting in a sauna or steam room can improve your circulation, ease muscle pain, and help with some skin problems. For water signs, taking a sauna is a great way to cleanse the soul and calm the mind. Look to see if a local gym or spa has one you can use. Sit and let the dry heat of the sauna or the hot steam of the steam room surround you and loosen the stress in your body.

If you don't have access to a steam room, you can create your own budget version by turning your shower on hot for a few minutes, shutting the door and windows, and letting the room fill with steam. Sit in a towel and enjoy the sensation of moisture floating all around you!

Take Ice-Skating Lessons

E ven frozen water has a special place in a water sign's heart. Just because you can't see the water moving and hear it lapping doesn't mean it is any less soothing or refreshing! In fact, ice can be invigorating for a water sign. Try embracing your cold side by taking beginners' ice-skating lessons. A number of world-class ice-skaters have been water signs. If you already have had some practice and aren't in the mood for a full lesson, try going to a local skating rink and just skate on your own for a little while. You may find that the smooth cut of the blade over ice soothes you.

Learn Something New

———————————

Mentally, water signs can understand a whole concept quickly because they intuitively feel it, rather than logically piece it together. The details are not important to them; all they need is to trust their gut and the emotions they are feeling inside. Their empathy is what helps them understand.

Use this superpower by learning something new—topics like philosophy and religion are a great place for water signs to start. These categories often require your ability to grasp a larger concept and understand things at a holistic level, rather than memorize detailed facts and figures. You may even find it beneficial to watch documentaries or listen to lectures in addition to reading a book—whatever sparks your passion!

Try a Boxing Workout

While water signs don't usually respond well to exercises that require a lot of repetition, a boxing workout is definitely an exception. In fact, a few world champion boxers over the years have been water signs. Boxing workouts are a great emotional and physical release if you've been feeling stressed or angry. The power and strength you'll feel when you learn with an expert to kick, punch, and duck properly will keep you coming back to the gym for more. Initially, you may find it difficult to get used to the new motions, but once your body adapts, boxing training is actually a very fluid activity, perfect for water signs! Look into beginners' classes in your local area.

Honor Eagles

The Eagle is Scorpio's second symbol (the other two being the Scorpion and the Phoenix). These beautiful birds are majestic and spirited, much like Scorpio herself. This bird represents spirit that can fly closer to the sun than any other—and yet also is a fierce hunter. The eagle can also represent Scorpio moving from the lower to the higher spiritual life.

Learn more about these regal animals. You may find that you identify with other qualities they possess. Consider putting their likeness in your home, or keeping a picture of an eagle in your desk drawer at work. Their strength and perseverance are wonderful reminders that you are stronger than you think, and capable of soaring to great heights.

Express Your Feelings

You feel so deeply, water sign, it's only natural that sometimes your emotions spill over and become overwhelming. Water signs are often receptive and inwardly focused. While you are very good at recognizing your feelings, you find it difficult to express them to others. You have trouble articulating what's inside. Instead, you would prefer that your loved ones just understand what you are feeling rather than having to explain it to them.

Practice expressing your emotions by keeping a journal. At least once a day, preferably at night after you've spent the day processing emotions, write down how you feel. If you are struggling with where to begin, start with the words *I feel* and go from there. Remember that no one will ever read this journal unless you want them to, so don't feel self-conscious. Just write what feels natural.

Indulge in Rainy Days

Some water signs prefer moody, cool, gray weather to bright sunshine. If you have the opportunity, indulge in a rainy day by staying inside, snuggling up on the couch, and listening to the rain beating down outside. You may choose to read a book or listen to music, whatever feels right. If you are feeling adventurous, you may even want to go for a walk in the rain. Make sure you have the right equipment—every water sign should have a decent raincoat and pair of rain boots. Check the weather forecast often to stay ahead of any potential rainy days.

Keep Photo Memories

Scrapbooks, photo albums, and iPhone picture galleries are all treasures to water signs. They love to flip through their favorite memories and reminisce about old times or relive their happiest moments.

Spend time putting together collections of photos that chronicle each part of your life. You can organize them in whatever way feels right to you. The goal is to make sure you are surrounded by your most cherished memories at all times. You may even consider putting together a photo collage that you can frame and hang on the wall. You can indulge your love of photos even further by creating a scrapbook or online photo book for your loved ones on their birthdays. The personal touch will bring tears and smiles.

Give Mastic a Try

———————

Mastic is a spice exclusively (it is true; the only place it grows is on Chios) found on the southern side of the Greek island of Chios. It has a pungent taste that Scorpio loves. While the tree that produces mastic is closely related to the pistachio, the flavor is a refreshing cedar or pine taste. Mastic has been used as a natural remedy for a range of discomforts, including many digestive ailments. Why not give it a try in some traditional Greek recipes? Better yet, take a trip to Chios to visit the home of this intriguing spice. While there, you can also tour medieval villages and visit beautiful beaches.

Embrace Your Sentimental Side

Whether they are celebrating birthdays, Christmas, or Valentine's Day, water signs love the holidays and any happy occasion. You especially love the sentimentality of tradition. Think about all the ways you can participate in holiday or birthday customs with the people you love. This may mean cooking a special meal for everyone, setting up decorations, or just spending time catching up with family and friends. Use your creative side to start new traditions, and encourage your loved ones to get involved. These rituals will help you feel closer to the people you cherish most.

Make Water a Part of Your Sleep Routine

While many water signs don't have trouble falling asleep, you may find that turning on a sound machine that features the sounds of rain, waves, or running water will make you feel more relaxed when you are drifting off to dreamland. Some water signs find that they are distracted by their emotions when they are trying to go to sleep. They replay things that happened throughout the day and relive how those things made them feel instead of quieting their minds. Sound machines can help focus your mind and ward off any distractions. Simply breathe deeply and listen to the sounds around you, and you'll be asleep in no time.

Stay Grounded

I t is important for water signs to live close to water
(or visit it as often as possible) as a way of staying
grounded. A view of some body of water from your
home window will orient you and keep you stable,
especially when you are feeling vulnerable or overwhelmed by your emotions. Seeing water can bring
balance to your life that you would otherwise miss.
The closer you can get to the water, the better. Watch
out for high-rise apartments, though, even if they
have a great view of water in the distance. Being up
high can make water signs feel lost and aimless, as if
they have no roots.

Decorate with Ocean Hues

Your home is a reflection of who you are and what you love. Water signs need a calming and soothing environment to thrive in, and the first way to accomplish this is to surround yourself with colors that are reminiscent of water. Look for muted, cool tones like light blue, gray, and deep green, accented with splashes of vibrant, warm colors like red and orange. You may even want to try painting a mural or pattern that makes you think of water on one of your walls. Above all, your home should be comfortable and familiar to you. Use color to make it your own.

Attend a Masquerade

O ne of Scorpio's ruling heavenly bodies is Pluto. In Greek mythology Pluto was called Hades, and one of his powers was granting the use of a helmet that made the wearer invisible. Scorpio would love to have such an object; she loves being enigmatic and does not like to reveal herself to others. If you can't have a helmet of invisibility, why not try for the next best thing, a disguise! and attend a masquerade ball?

These balls are mysterious and sometimes romantic, both of which appeal to Scorpio. So, if you're looking for a fun night out that is suited to your astrological tendencies, attend a masquerade ball. If you can't find one near you, host your own!

Buy an Aquarium

J ust because you don't live right next to a body of water doesn't mean you can't make the aquatic a part of your everyday life. One of the easiest ways to bring the ocean home is to invest in an aquarium. As a water sign, you'll find solace in the cool blue ripples of the water and the fluid movement of the fish swimming by. It's true that keeping a healthy aquarium does require research, advice from experts, money, and time, but the cost is well worth the benefits you'll see almost instantly in your mood.

Try Your Hand at Cartooning

Creative and humorous, cartoons can be both a source of humor and a thought-provoking statement on current affairs. If you find that you enjoy reading cartoons, why not try creating your own?

Drawing cartoons and writing witty captions will appeal to Scorpio's sense of humor and creativity. Not only that, but the act itself is a productive and cathartic form of self-care. No matter your talent level, cartooning is a worthwhile hobby to look into.

Host a Murder Mystery Night

———————

Scorpio is the sign of all things mysterious. Feed your creativity and create a true mystery by hosting a murder mystery night.

Whether you create the mystery yourself or buy a package from a website like www.mymysteryparty.com, this is a great opportunity to flex your creative side, unwind, and socialize with friends. To ensure that the evening maintains an authentic, secretive energy, invite guests who share your creativity and love of mystery. Assign roles ahead of time so that guests can arrive already in character. Not only will this evening be thrilling and fun, but you will stimulate your brain in a wonderful way—an unorthodox yet exciting act of self-care.

Create Your Own Water Feature

———————

R unning water is soothing to water signs at work and at home. Purchase a small water fountain that you can keep near your desk at work to help you through stressful moments. When you are feeling overwhelmed, take a few moments to focus on the sound of the water and nothing else. You can leave the fountain running all day to help keep you feeling balanced and calm. If you have space at home, purchase another water fountain for your living room, or wherever you spend the most time. The trickling water will keep you company whenever you need it.

Spending time outdoors is also beneficial for water signs, so look for a water fountain that can be set up on a deck or in your backyard.

Don't Go to the Desert

Dry climates don't suit water signs well. You need to feel moisture in the air in order to breathe easy. While it's not advisable for water signs to live in a dry climate like the desert, if you do, there are certain things you can try to keep the air around you moist. The easiest is to research and purchase a humidifier for your home and run it as needed. This will significantly improve the quality of the air.

You can also look for an essential oil diffuser that uses water, which not only adds moisture to the air, but also diffuses essential oils to impact your mood. Experiment with different scents to find the one that is right for you.

Cherish Family Heirlooms

Family is very important to you as a water sign. You take comfort in the familial connections you have, and take pride in your loyalty to family no matter what. Because of this, your bond to your family only grows stronger day by day.

Every family is unique and has their own collection of heirlooms that are passed down from generation to generation. Display your own family heirlooms proudly. They are a special link to your ancestors and show off who you truly are.

Spice Things Up!

Give your dishes some kick by adding horseradish. The great thing about horseradish is that it doesn't just deliver a spicy zing, which Scorpio enjoys, it's also packed with a number of beneficial minerals and nutrients, including calcium, potassium, magnesium, and zinc. It's the perfect ingredient for a simple home-made salad dressing, it provides a great bite when spread on a burger, and it adds the right amount of heat to your Bloody Mary.

By adding horseradish to your dishes, you're fighting inflammation, helping with digestion, and protecting against bacteria as it has antimicrobial properties. It's the perfect addition for the Scorpio who's seeking some spice.

Learn to Dance the Tango

Dance in any form is an intimate expression of the dancer's feelings. The tango is the perfect dance for Scorpio as it puts your sensual side on display, allowing you to channel your inner desires through movement. The dance creates a connection between the partners and allows for an exciting intimacy that you can continue off the dance floor.

If you have a partner, sign up for a couples' class and learn together. If you're single, you can still bring the heat and have some fun, learning alongside others who are looking to master the dance as well. It's a fun way to exercise and get your heart rate going—and depending on your connection with your partner, it may even get your heart racing!

Surround Yourself
with Succulents

_____

Succulents are some of the easiest plants to care for—some can grow well in indoor environments and require less frequent watering. These are the perfect plants for a busy water sign. Jade is a particularly popular choice—it is known as the lucky tree, or the money tree, and needs very little care to thrive. The color of the flowers that bloom from the plant can be either pink or white. Not only are succulents beautiful to look at, but surrounding yourself with green is a great way to reduce stress and create a calming, nurturing environment. Succulents can also increase productivity and concentration, so consider placing one near your workstation as well.

Meditate Alone

Spiritual practices such as meditation are best done alone for water signs. That's because meditation is a time of emotional vulnerability, and water signs are highly sensitive to other people's energies. If you are meditating with a group, you may inadvertently absorb other people's feelings rather than focus on your own. Instead, find a comfortable, private area where you can let your guard down and feel safe. Make sure your meditation spot is relaxing and inviting, with a soft seat and soothing ambiance. It may help to listen to quiet music or put on a sound machine to keep you focused.

Chase Your Wanderlust

Sticking close to home is a comfort for many water signs. It's okay to prefer staying in to going out, but you should try to challenge your homebody habit by booking a trip somewhere far away every now and again. You may initially feel anxious about being away from home, but the excitement of seeing far-off, different lands may outweigh the discomfort. The good news is, as long as the room you stay in while traveling is comfortable, you'll be able to feel safe. Water signs just need a secure place to rest their heads, and they'll be able to enjoy new places without too much worry.

Keep Your Mind Sharp

S corpio needs a keen mind in order to stay quick with her wit and her words. As Scorpio's mind is always moving, reading people and probing situations, it's important to keep those skills sharp—they're one of Scorpio's best assets, after all.

An entertaining way to exercise these mental muscles is by picking up a book of riddles and brainteasers. Set aside some time to stretch your analytical skills and solve the puzzles included in the collection. You'll find the same reasoning and logic you use in the real world put to the test in a fun, engaging way.

Kick-Start Your Day with Coffee

A good cup of strong coffee is the perfect start to any Scorpio's day. This no-nonsense sign is serious about her morning joe and enjoys a straight-forward cup to get her going.

Find a purveyor of straight-from-the-source coffee beans instead of something you might pick up in your local supermarket. The intense flavor will complement your own intensity. Rather than simply throwing a pot on or using an instant coffee appliance, turn the process into a ritual. Take a moment to enjoy the aroma of the coffee as it brews, don't cheat the taste with too much creamer or sweetener, and enjoy the cup of coffee from the first sip to the last.

Adopt a Dog or Cat

The world is broken up into dog people and cat people. While there are many people who enjoy both types of domesticated animals, they usually have a preference for one over the other. Water signs are definitely more cat people, but have been known to fall in love with small dogs as well.

Cats are independent and curious, traits that water signs appreciate. Small dogs can be outgoing and rambunctious (depending on their breed), also characteristics that appeal to a sometimes moody water sign. The key for water signs is finding a small animal to share your space with, one that fits well into the home you've already created for yourself. Just make sure to get expert advice on adopting (and properly caring for) your chosen pet from a local animal shelter before you commit.

Spend Time with Loved Ones

E ven though water signs are homebodies, they do like to socialize when the environment is just right. This usually means hanging out with a small group of close family members or friends. Water signs need to be surrounded by people they trust to feel comfortable enough to kick back and relax.

If you aren't in the mood to venture out beyond your front door, consider inviting your friends or family over for a small dinner party where you can all enjoy one another's company and speak candidly about your thoughts and emotions. This is a water sign's dream get-together!

Take a Dip in a Mud Bath

Why not get dirty to get clean? The many cleansing and detoxifying properties of mud baths make them an amazing spa day treat for Scorpio. It's a transformational experience of heated water and earth that relaxes your body, soothes your muscles, and exfoliates your skin. Scorpio will emerge from the bath refreshed and ready to take on the world.

Find a spa close to you that offers mud baths, and book yourself some time to enjoy the treatment. Try to make a full day of it, as you don't want to unwind only to tense up afterward due to a tight schedule. If you can't sneak away for a full day or find a mud bath treatment in your area, research and buy a luxurious mud mask online and enjoy it on a smaller scale at home.

Take In a Concert

Live music is invigorating for many water signs. While being in crowds can sometimes be overwhelming for them, the positive energy of the music can help them overcome that discomfort. There's nothing quite like singing along to one of your favorite songs live. Surrender to the spirit of the music and let it permeate your being.

If you have the opportunity, look for an outdoor concert where you can combine your love of nature with the power of live music. During the summer months you'll find outdoor music festivals popping up all over the world that attract a variety of artists and fans. Find one that speaks to your unique musical taste!

Try Bach's Holly Remedy

There's an intensity to Scorpio that burns bright and provides strength to those born under this Sun sign. Sometimes, though, Scorpio's passion can burn a little too bright and may benefit from some calming. One option to ease this intensity is the original Bach Flower Remedies, which are made from wildflowers and, according to the company, "gently restore the balance between mind and body."

Bach's holly remedy is meant to help those who are "attacked by thoughts of such kind as jealousy, envy, revenge, suspicion," which can sometimes be the case for Scorpio. If and when you do feel yourself in such a state, try adding a couple of drops of holly to a glass of water (follow the directions on the bottle) and drinking slowly. (The Bach Flower Remedies are available online.)

Dine on Natural Aphrodisiacs

As Scorpio rules the reproductive organs, it's only natural for those born under the sign to have a heightened sexual energy. When Scorpio wants to turn up the heat, she's very capable on her own—but indulging in some natural aphrodisiacs can increase desire for all parties involved.

Next time you're planning a romantic night, find a high-quality restaurant that specializes in shellfish and order a dozen oysters for you and your date (as long as neither of you is allergic to shellfish). The zinc and amino acids (which increase dopamine) will aid in arousal.

You may also want to have some saffron ice cream in your freezer for when you return home. The spice is another known aphrodisiac, and the ice cream will cool things down before you heat things up.

Attend the Ballet or Opera

As a water sign, you are driven by emotion and feeling. This is why you may feel such an inherent draw toward the performing arts, like dance and theater. Indulge this love by attending a ballet or opera performance in your area. Ballet is a beautiful example of the fluidity of motion, which speaks to water signs on a visceral level, and opera presents a vivid story through the power of song and language. Attending the opera can be a very emotional experience for the audience, so bring your tissues, water sign!

Embrace Your Love of History

Water signs love to travel to different times in their imaginations—that's why historical fiction is the perfect genre for this literary sign. Why not turn that love of different time periods into an excuse to actually visit those historical sites?

Make a list of sites that you have always wanted to see, and start visiting. Studying history requires that you imagine yourself in the same situations as the people of that time. As a water sign, you are incredibly empathetic and understanding, so this skill probably comes easily to you. Use it to your advantage and relive some of the most important moments in history with your own eyes.

Investigate Your Past Lives

Who's to say we only have one life to live? For those who believe our souls have inhabited other bodies and lived other lives, a past-life reading is a potential way to unlock the histories and mysteries of those lives gone before. Scorpio's interest in mysticism and spirituality allows for an openness to this type of believing—at least enough to question and investigate if it's true.

There may be something more to that old familiar feeling, and there's one way to get to the bottom of it. After doing your research and receiving recommendations from a trusted source, visit a past-life expert and have a reading. See what memories from your former lives can be recalled and how those past lives can affect your present and future.

Trust Your Intuition

Do you sometimes find that you intuitively know what time it is without even checking your watch or phone? That's because water signs have a great internal sense of time. You're probably always early to your appointments, and don't even need to set an alarm to wake up in the morning.

Learn to trust your intuition more in all parts of your life, not just when it comes to being on time. As a water sign, you can usually trust your gut instinct. You have a talent for reading situations and people through how you feel. This is a strength that you can rely on. Don't second-guess yourself so much—learn to listen to that voice in your mind. It's usually right!

Go to Therapy

While water signs have a lot of emotions swirling around inside, classic therapy might not work for them. They don't like to get stuck living in the past, mulling over things that have already happened. To them, the past is a bottomless well of memory. When it comes to talking about their feelings, they prefer to focus on targeted problems. However, they can certainly benefit from the journey.

If you are considering therapy, ask your doctor for recommendations, and then look around for a therapist who understands exactly what you are looking to get out of your sessions. It may take some trial and error, but eventually you'll find the right professional and right approach for you.

Depend on Your Water Friends

Sometimes, in order to really work through a problem, you need to turn to someone who just intuitively understands you. For water signs this means seeking out other water signs. They are usually just as good at listening as you are, and can help you work through whatever is going on in your life at the time. Since water signs are so sympathetic, they will always be around to lend an ear when you need it. It is important for water signs to support one another, especially when it comes to their emotional health and balance.

Open Yourself Up to Spiritual Study

There's a difference between religious and spiritual. As someone who is in touch with her spiritual side, Scorpio recognizes and appreciates that difference, and finds herself looking to deepen her understanding of her spiritual leanings. It's through fully understanding and appreciating a spiritual ritual or belief that Scorpio will adopt it and incorporate it into her life.

Is there a spiritual practice that has always piqued your interest? If so, delve into its origins, discover the power it possesses, and, if it truly speaks to you, make it a part of your life. You are in charge of your own spirituality, and you can incorporate it as you see fit.

Chant Your Way to Calm

As a water sign, you may become easily overwhelmed by a lot of noise, but chanting may have the reverse effect on you if you are looking to relax and zen out. For centuries Buddhist monks have used chanting as a way to prepare the mind for meditation. You, too, can use this ritual to find peace. Repetitive chanting often mimics the ebb and flow of water, something that innately pleases water signs. Try researching a few chants that you can use in the comfort of your own home. When you are ready to meditate, start chanting, and repeat the words over and over again until a sense of calm sweeps over you.

Try White Magic

Have you ever cast a spell? As an intense and transformative person, you may find that a simple white ("good") magic spell may help you feel empowered. While it is important to limit spellcasting to white magic to avoid hurting anyone, consider how magic could help you create meaningful life changes.

If you are looking to manifest a change in your personal or professional life, research a spell that could help move the needle. *The Modern Witchcraft Spell Book* by Skye Alexander offers beginner spells you could try, or you can look online for a spell to help you reach a specific goal. Regardless of which spell you choose, be sure to keep your intentions pure, and enjoy the experience as an emotional and mental act of self-care.

Get Lost in a Good Mystery

Time spent with a good book is time well spent. By setting aside some time to read, you are allowing yourself to relax while still keeping your mind sharp. Scorpio isn't one to sit on the sidelines though, and a good mystery book makes her an active participant. You'll enjoy trying to solve the mystery ahead of the characters and staying a step ahead of the author's intended misdirections and red herrings. The probing and insight you use in the real world will serve you well as the lead detective in the latest page-turner. And as a Scorpio, you can tend to be a bit of a mystery yourself, so you may learn a thing or two.

Meditate with Crystals

mploying the help of the right crystal at the right time can do wonders for balancing your energy and emotions. Look for crystals that are reminiscent of the ocean, such as blue lace agate, aquamarine, and lapis lazuli. Blue lace agate can calm anxiety and worry, aquamarine promotes courage and communication, and lapis lazuli can help you discover the truth about yourself and your life. When you are meditating, hold the crystal of your choosing in your hand or close to your heart. Use its energy and power to achieve your goals, no matter what they are.

Explore Your Artistic Side

Water signs are instinctively very artistic. Tap into your creative side by trying a new craft, such as watercolor painting. Watercolors are a more forgiving medium for novice painters than oil paints. Try painting ocean scenes, waterfalls, or lakes. The act of painting can be very soothing for the artist. If you are struggling at first, you may find it helps to look at an image to replicate as you paint, or purchase an acrylic paint-by-numbers kit. Once you've gotten the hang of brushstrokes and color blending, you can create an original piece.

Hone Your Photography Skills

As a water sign, you have incredible observation skills and an eye for beauty. This makes you the ideal photographer. You are able to identify poignancy in any scene, and isolate it with the perfect shot. You also love to keep copies of all the photographs you take so you can revisit these moments whenever you want.

To enhance your photography skills, consider investing in a high-quality camera with digital capabilities. This way you can have a digital record of your work, in addition to prints. Before you purchase, do some research to find out which camera will be best for you and your skill level.

Pamper Yourself

Pampering yourself is essential for any self-care routine. For water signs this means spending time focusing on their outer appearance as well as their inner wellness. Dedicate time to indulging yourself with a spa facial. Facials are great for increasing circulation in your facial muscles and hydrating the skin. They can also decrease puffiness and slow the formation of wrinkles.

If you don't have the budget to pay for a spa-level facial, you can always try at-home masks. Many of these masks are made from ingredients that are already in your pantry or refrigerator, such as cucumber. Research which kind of mask will work best for your skin type.

Flavor Your Water

———

You already know that drinking enough water is one key to good health, but this is especially true for water signs. You need to ingest enough water every day to keep your body strong. Staying hydrated doesn't have to be boring, though. Hydrating with water is by far the best option, but you can spice things up by adding a few ingredients to make your own flavored water. Try stirring in a few strawberries or raspberries, or just add a splash of lemon juice or cucumbers to your water pitcher. Not only do these ingredients brighten the flavor of your water, but many of them have antioxidant properties that can boost your immune system.

Protect Yourself from Energy Vampires

Water signs feel deeply and can easily be drained by emotionally manipulative people. Trust your gut when it comes to whom you spend your time with. If you find that someone is particularly toxic to you or you feel that your energy is depleted after seeing them, consider removing them from your life. As a water sign, you need to care for your emotional wellness and protect yourself against energy vampires. If you are feeling particularly vulnerable, try carrying around a piece of rose quartz to buffer against negativity. Wearing the crystal as a necklace near your heart is even better.

Show Off Another Time Period

If you love a particular historical period, consider decorating part of your home with objects from that era. Because of their empathetic abilities, water signs are able to build worlds in their minds that they can visit every now and again. Bridge the gap between your reality and imagination by surrounding yourself with objects that remind you of another time and place. You could create an American Civil War room, an ancient Egyptian room, or a Viking room.

If you are more in love with a certain place than a time period, apply the same principle. Collect objects from that area and put them on display.

Go for an Aqua Jog

———

A lot of people assume Scorpio is a fire sign; it may be because Mars is one of her ruling planets, or it may be due to her passionate personality. However, as you know, Scorpio is a water sign and the pool is a great place to get your exercise. Swimming laps isn't the only option though. Scorpio's determined demeanor makes aqua jogging another perfect form of in-pool workout.

Aqua jogging is a great cardiovascular activity, like its on-land counterpart, but by exercising in the pool, you cut down on the stress on your joints. So, next time you're looking for a fun way to de-stress, buckle into a buoyancy belt and break a sweat in the pool.

Write a Story

Your imagination is expansive as a water sign. You have the gift of creation, seamlessly moving between reality and the made-up worlds in your mind. Some of the best writers working today are water signs, so try putting your visions down on paper and sharing them with the world. Start small by writing a short story, or even just the beginning paragraphs of a larger project. Live inside your own imagination for a while and see what comes forth. Remember that not every sentence you write needs to be perfect. Just focus on expressing your ideas, and you can go back and revise what you've already written later on.

Volunteer

_____

In nature inactive water becomes stagnant and attracts bacteria. Water needs to run, gurgle, babble, and sway. Water signs are the same way. Doing nothing can make a water sign feel useless and bored. To quench your desire to be active and helpful, volunteer at an organization that you care about deeply. Play with dogs at a shelter, read to children at the library, or make lunches for the homeless. For you, being active doesn't just mean moving your body; it also means spending your time meaningfully. These small acts can change the world!

Join a Club

_____

Water signs love to be included in groups, even though they can sometimes get overwhelmed by too many people. The sense of belonging is important for them to feel appreciated and loved. The key for you as a water sign is to find a small group that focuses on something you really love. This could be a book club that meets once a month, a cooking class, or a wildlife club that goes on adventures in nature. There will be no shortage of interesting conversation; you'll find loads to talk about with people who share your loves.

Keep a Dream Diary

Water signs have notoriously vivid dreams that stick with them after waking. You may even dream of future events, or have trouble deciphering if what happened was a dream or reality.

Try keeping a dream diary to chronicle all of the dreams you remember. When you wake up and the dream is fresh in your mind, take a few minutes to write down key words that describe the dream. Ask yourself some questions: How did you feel? Who was there? What was happening? The more detail you can put on paper, the better able you'll be to interpret the dreams later on.

Get Back in Black—Head to Toe

———————

Dressing well is not always about looking good, it's about feeling good. Luckily, Scorpio knows how to feel good while looking good. Why not embrace your dark side while doing so? Next time you're getting ready to go out on the town, opt for an all-black outfit, and give it even more of an edge by working in at least one leather (real or faux) accessory or article of clothing—whether it's boots or a belt, a skirt or pants. It's not that you necessarily need the confidence boost that comes with such an ensemble, but it's just one more way to embody the mysteriously seductive Scorpio. Now you can look good, feel good, and be bad.

Have Yourself a Stinger

———————————

While it's a reference to the venomous appendage of a scorpion, the stinger is also the perfect cocktail for Scorpio, as the minty mixture makes for a pointed libation. As an after-dinner drink, the stinger is a perfect way to segue into your next nighttime activity—whatever that may be.

Here's your simple recipe for a stinger: 2 ounces brandy and ¾ ounce white crème de menthe. Shake ingredients with ice and strain into a rocks glass with ice.

Soar in Eagle Pose

While Scorpio is tied closely to its Scorpion symbol, the Eagle is also a symbol of the sign. The Eagle Pose lets you work on your balance while improving blood flow. This is not a beginners' pose, so make sure to practice this with your yoga instructor for technique guidance.

To begin, stand in Mountain Pose (standing straight, feet together, arms by your side). Bend the hips, knees, and ankles. Cross the left leg over the right thigh and wrap the top of your left foot around the right calf as best you can. Bring your arms to the center in front of you and entwine them, crossing the right elbow over the inside of the left elbow. Bend your elbows. Turn the palms to face each other and join them. Lift the elbows to shoulder height and move the forearms away from the face to bring the wrists over the elbows. Gaze straight ahead. Remain in the pose for several breaths, and then repeat on the other side.

Start a Collection

Since water signs feel at home near bodies of water, it makes sense for them to pick up pieces of those water sources with them wherever they go. Start collecting stones, rocks, or shells from every body of water you visit. The energy of the water will stay within these objects and help keep you balanced when you are on dry land. When you are feeling lost, sit quietly and hold each object in your hands. Feel the positive vibrations radiating from them. If you'd like, you can create an altar of your water objects in your bedroom to help attract calm thoughts while you drift off to dreamland. Or, when you are in need of an energy boost, put one in your purse or pocket so you can hold it whenever you want as you go about your day.

Repeat Your Mantra

S corpio is the strongest sign in the zodiac when it comes to transforming herself. As a bold, empowered Scorpio, you have the ability to transcend your current state and evolve. If you find yourself in a place where you need to be reminded of that strength and ability, recite the mantra "I transform my life."

When you repeat this phrase, focus on where you want to be in life. Do not focus on what's holding you back. You are a strong, determined Scorpio; if you believe in this mantra and put it out into the universe, you will transform your life.

Try Patchouli Essential Oil

———

Patchouli oil has myriad benefits, many of which will serve Scorpio well. As a natural antidepressant, patchouli oil can lighten your mood and relieve stress. While Scorpio may not be depressed, her intense nature could benefit from the scent of some essential oil. The peaceful properties of patchouli will be able to calm you down after a particularly trying day.

The aroma of this essential oil has also been used as a natural aphrodisiac for hundreds of years; it can be used to boost your sex drive and ease any sexual anxieties. As Scorpio rules the reproductive organs, adding some patchouli oil to a diffuser in the bedroom is a great way to get—and keep—things going.

Keep Hematite Close

The dark hematite stone—a mysterious stone for a mysterious sign—is the mineral form of iron oxide and contains healing properties that work well for Scorpio. Hematite is often used to help ground people and clear negative emotions. Since Scorpio can sometimes let her emotions get the better of her, hematite is perfect to keep on hand to clear those toxic feelings and remain levelheaded.

It's important to keep hematite close by when you are in situations that may trigger negative emotions—whether those are feelings of jealousy, anger, or frustration. Keep hematite on your desk if you feel those feelings flare at work, or have some on your bedside table to help remove negative thoughts before bed.

Get Yourself a Scorpion

A pet scorpion? That is a little much, even for you, fearless Scorpio. But you can still keep a totem of your Sun sign's symbol—maybe a small figurine or a scorpion in amber—nearby as a source of strength. Scorpions have been around for millions of years in one form or another—adapting and adjusting to the world around them to survive, similar to Scorpio herself.

While a fierce predator who can pack a punch with their venomous stinger, the Scorpion symbolizes the unevolved form of Scorpio, the one who can do damage to herself with too much excess—whether that's too much drinking or extreme dieting, or some other destructive behavior. A scorpion totem can act as a reminder of who you can become if you're not careful and remind you to take care of yourself rather than suffer your own sting.

Visit a Hot Spring

While a hot bath is always nice and relaxing, Scorpio could use something a little more exciting than warm water in her bathroom. Why settle for a hot bath when you can enjoy a hot spring? As a water sign with a hot temper (occasionally), Scorpio is well suited to bathing in a hot spring. The water is heated naturally by the earth and can contain a number of beneficial minerals like calcium, magnesium, potassium, and zinc—meaning your dip will help relieve stress, smooth your skin, increase circulation, and more. Research the health considerations of hot springs before you go.

If you're not within driving distance of a hot spring, plan a trip and make it an all-natural adventure. You deserve a break, and this will soothe your body and your soul.

Do Something Daring

———————

Scorpio is known for being bold, but sometimes you need to remind yourself of that fact. It's healthy to test your limits and try something new. What other people consider daring is probably a little everyday for you, Scorpio. You need to find something that will push you out of your comfort zone. What about a trip to a nudist resort? Or lessons in windsurfing? Or something else that might make others blush, or back away in fear? The goal isn't to be uncomfortable to the point of not participating though; it's about pushing boundaries. Choose something you'll ultimately enjoy, but that will be a thrill while you're doing it.

Give Yourself a Scare

S ome people turn to their favorite comedies when they need to relax. Others get lost in an old Hollywood classic. Scorpio though? Bring on the horror movies—the darker, the better. Scorpio has an interest in the macabre and the mysterious, making horror movies an obvious go-to, whether you're looking to stay in and *Netflix* and chill or take in an all-night horror-fest.

There are actually also some health benefits to all the jumps and scares—not that Scorpio scares easily. A study funded by a UK movie subscription service found that watching horror movies can actually burn calories; the study's participants burned 184 calories while watching *The Shining*.

Try Clove Tea

C love, the aromatic spice from Asia, works twofold for Scorpio, who rules over both the elimination and reproductive organs. Cloves may help the digestive system and alleviate gas. And cloves are also known to be a natural aphrodisiac. While these are two separate benefits, the fact that cloves can accomplish both makes it the perfect spice for Scorpio to select after dinner. Before you do so, check with your doctor (who is familiar with your health and medications).

A simple way to make a clove tea is by adding a teaspoon of ground cloves to boiling water. You can include other spices if you desire. Let it steep for 15 minutes, strain, and serve. Whether you're looking for relief or action, the cloves will work their magic.

Visit a Graveyard

There's a connection between Scorpio and the afterlife. Being ruled by Pluto, the celestial body named for the god of the underworld, Scorpio has a proclivity for the other side. It's not something to be ashamed or afraid of though, as a powerful link to the afterlife allows for greater knowledge here on earth. By taking a respectful and reflective walk through a graveyard, you're honoring your connection to Pluto as well as the souls of those who've passed.

If you're able to track down and travel to a graveyard of your ancestors, bring a sheet of paper and some rubbing wax or a crayon to make a gravestone rubbing. It's a sentimental connection to your past. Just be sure rubbings are allowed in the cemetery and you remain respectful during your visit.

Hula for Your Health

An ancient Polynesian dance form passed down generation by generation, hula is as much about storytelling as it is about movement. Each move helps to tell a greater story while getting your heart rate going, your hips and other joints moving, and your mind focused. It's a low-impact exercise that can work your entire body, and it's perfect for Scorpio who prefers there to be an intention behind her moves.

Check out your local gyms and cultural centers to see if they offer any hula exercise classes. If there aren't any classes held locally, you can find many beginners' instructional videos online.

Embrace Your Inner Phoenix

While Scorpio is most immediately identified by the Scorpion symbol, it's only the first of her three symbols. Whereas the Scorpion is the start of the sign's evolution and the Eagle symbolizes the transitional period, the Phoenix is the symbol of its complete transformation. The mythological bird is the embodiment of Scorpio's journey from darkness to light. No matter where you are on your own path, it's important to keep this symbol in sight. Look for a piece of art depicting the phoenix in flight, or perhaps a pin or carving; whatever you end up choosing, the importance is the meaning—you are the Phoenix and you will rise.

Kick a Bad Habit

Scorpio is extreme. This can be extremely beneficial for Scorpio, or it can be extremely detrimental. Unfortunately, in the case of vices, this extreme nature can be quite detrimental. Scorpio's bad habit isn't a once in a while type of thing. It often leads to too much—too much smoking, too much drinking, too much junk food, whatever the particular tendency. The good news to this black-and-white behavior is that once Scorpio sets her mind to it, she'll be extremely determined to stop.

You know what you need to stop doing. It can be risky behavior or negative thinking. Whatever it is, make a plan on how to overcome it, and stick with it. Turn that darkness into light.

Be Cautious of Secrets

Some signs are sunny extroverts who want everyone to know everything about them at all times. Not Scorpio though. While Scorpio is a deeply devoted friend, she enjoys keeping an air of mystery and a bit of distance between herself and other people. Such a secretive side keeps people guessing and crafts an enigmatic persona, welcomed by this sign ruled by Pluto.

Embrace your mystery, but don't let it wall you off from other people. As you know, when you do connect with others, you forge a strong connection. Allow people to see you for the fiercely loyal friend you can be—even if you have a secret or two.

Practice Deep Meditation

Scorpio isn't looking for 5 minutes of mindfulness or 10 minutes of sitting peacefully to practice breathing exercises. No, Scorpio is searching for meaningful transformation and is willing to work for it. Your focus should be on transforming the darkness into light and then carrying that lightness with you. Scorpio likes to live in the extremes, so a next-level meditative practice makes sense.

Deep meditation is its own practice in itself. In order to start practicing deep meditation effectively, you should look up a recommended class or follow instructions from a trusted teacher's app or online courses.

Try Garlic for Health

I n the winter, our bodies often require assistance to stay healthy. Boost your immunity and add a dash of flavor to your meals by increasing your raw garlic intake.

At first, try grating it on salads or adding it to other dishes. Work your way up to consuming a half clove. If you don't like the taste, try garlic extract in the capsule form.

As with any new health regimen, consult your physician before trying.

Give Muay Thai a Try

***

Scorpio likes her workouts to be as intense as her personality. What better way to get an intense workout than by training in this combat sport? Muay Thai is a sport from Thailand that's made its way around the world as both a fighting style and an exercise opportunity. Similar to a scorpion's stinging strike, Muay Thai is built around a combination of strikes delivered from the "eight limbs," or the eight points of contact allowed: hands, shins, elbows, and knees.

To exercise with Muay Thai, you don't necessarily need to get in the ring and square off against an opponent—though that might be welcomed some days. You can look for a beginners' workout class with expert coaches in your area that teaches the boxing-martial art hybrid, and ask the trainer to adapt the practice to your needs and fitness.

Balance Your Root Chakra

Chakras are spinning energy centers that directly influence your well-being, and how consciously and happily you create your life's path. There are seven chakras in your body, starting with the first chakra, or the root chakra. This is located at the base of your spine and is in charge of grounding you. When your root chakra is out of balance, you can find yourself feeling aggressive and reckless. Given Scorpio's tendency to fall victim to those kinds of feelings, it's a good idea to try and balance your root chakra.

One of the best ways to balance your chakras is by visiting an energy healer. A Reiki healer can identify whether or not your chakras are out of balance and then aim to transfer energy to heal the imbalance.

Add Probiotics to Your Diet

While Scorpio is better known for ruling over the reproductive system, she also rules over the elimination organs. As important as the mouth is to the digestive process so too are these body parts. Scorpio's governance over this particular part of the tract means she should be mindful of what she does and doesn't eat. Try adding probiotics into your diet; these microorganisms found in different foods help balance the good and bad bacteria in your system and will help with digestion and elimination.

Foods and drinks to try that are rich in probiotics include yogurt, pickles, and kimchi. Probiotics are an easy way to be good to your digestive system. If you are suffering from any health conditions, check with your doctor first.

Watch That Sarcastic Sting

Scorpions have their stingers, and Scorpio has her wit. It keeps her entertained and people laughing—until they're not. Occasionally, Scorpio can go a little too far, so it's best to keep your sarcastic comments in check. You're a water sign, after all, and are very in tune with others' emotions, so hurting them and setting fire to a bridge will ultimately hurt you.

Like a scorpion's stinger though, your wit is your best defense. Keep it sharp! Just know when to use it.

Embrace Spontaneity

We can all benefit from a little spontaneity in our lives. Changing things up and throwing ourselves a curveball can help keep us on our toes. Scorpio can do such a good job at structuring her day-to-day tasks that she can schedule any excitement or enjoyment out of her life. For a sign that loves a good thrill, creating such a rigid schedule can ruin that flow of energy and crush that Scorpio spirit.

Don't get stuck in a rut. Be open to changing things up—go out for dinner and drinks on a Tuesday. Take the long way home from work and stop for a treat. Start driving on a Saturday and see where the road takes you. Switch it up!

Help Others Evolve

It's true: by helping others, you can help yourself. As a Scorpio your role in the world is to help others evolve. You're a deeply intuitive spirit whose connections with others can help them grow and transcend their current state, especially if they are stuck. This guidance not only benefits the other person, it benefits you as well. Creating this type of spiritual connection with another person will help you develop your own sense of self. It also breaks down the wall you can sometimes build to the outside world. Help others find out the cause of their problems by asking questions and sharing your confidence.

Remember, though, not everyone is as determined as you are, Scorpio. Guiding others along this path will be a good lesson in patience.

Create a Scorpio Sanctuary

You are a passionate soul, Scorpio, who likes a little danger. Your living space should reflect that part of your personality. Home décor isn't just decoration, it's an expression of who you are and helps to make you feel at peace in your place. Blacks and deep burgundies are great colors for your bedroom and can be punctuated with bright whites and reds. These color choices speak to your mysterious yet sensual persona.

Even if this color palette isn't exactly right for your home, you can still sneak a little Scorpio into your décor. Pyramid paperweights are great for your desk—whether at home or at the office; the shape is harmonious with Scorpio power. You can also add a little danger to your living room with snakeskin patterned pillows, or maybe even a Venus flytrap plant. It's up to you how far you take it, but the most important thing is to make your space your own.

Find Power from Your Planets

S corpio is ruled by two different planets: Mars and Pluto. You can draw strength from both. Mars can be visible from earth during close approaches between the planets. At those times the planet burns bright in the night sky and is visible by the naked eye. Find out online the next time Mars will be on one of these close approaches, and then plan a night under the stars. Burn bright like the red planet, Scorpio.

And while Pluto may not be visible by the naked eye (and may not technically be a planet), you can still draw on its energy. Pluto's still a bit of a mystery—like you. Embrace that enigmatic power to keep people guessing.

Train for a Marathon

As a strong-willed Scorpio, you are a natural competitor who likes to push your own limits. If team sports are not your thing, try giving long-distance running a shot. By setting a goal of running a marathon, you'll only have yourself to compete with. Training can be tough, but you're built for this, Scorpio. Your determination will be your fuel as you run those 26.2 miles. Beyond the physical benefits of the exercise, the personal achievement of setting and accomplishing a goal like this will be a thrilling reward. Push yourself to the max!

Investigate Pendulum Power

Refine your innate transformative abilities by purchasing a pendulum in a stone or metal of your choosing.

Historically, the pendulum has been used as a way of gaining spiritual insight. It can provide you with healing and spiritual growth as it locates blocks in energy. By asking questions of the pendulum, you can receive guidance and awareness to clear your body and spirit.

It's important to understand what the swings of a pendulum can mean, so be sure to purchase your pendulum from a reputable business, and seek guidance on its proper use through an instructor or a book on pendulum dowsing.

Have Fun—but Be Safe

There's a sexual energy possessed by Scorpio that the other signs just can't match. It's not your fault that you were granted this gift, and you shouldn't feel any shame in enjoying it. However, it's important for you and your partner to always be safe. Take the necessary steps to ensure that your adventures in (and out of) the bedroom don't put either of you at risk—and then enjoy! Try out new positions, locations, and situations; spice things up any way you want. Embrace this prowess and let the physical manifestation of your passion deepen your connection.

Beware the Sting
of Stubbornness

Scorpio's strong will suits you well in many endeavors. However, if you're not careful, that strong will can sometimes become a stubborn streak. Don't let stubbornness get the best of you. You have too much to share with the world to wall yourself off from it. It's important to be open to other people's opinions even if they contradict your own. Rather than write a person off in that situation, allow yourself the opportunity to discuss your viewpoint, and then hear them out on theirs. You're very sharp, Scorpio, and you know when you're right—but it's wrong to let a disagreement ruin a relationship.